Florida-Backroads-Travel.com

SOUTHWEST FLORIDA BACKROADS TRAVEL

Second Edition, 2017

Copyright@2015-2017 – D. Michael "Mike" Miller

All Rights Reserved

CONTENTS

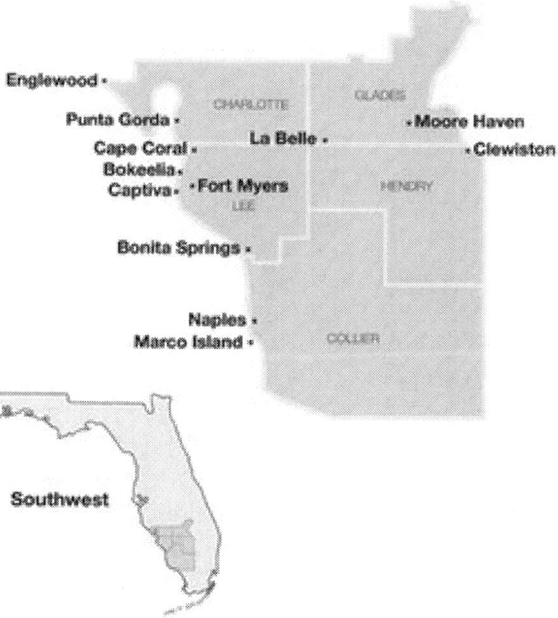

Englewood ·

Punta Gorda ·

Cape Coral ·

Bokeelia ·

Captiva · · Fort Myers

CHARLOTTE

GLADES

· Moore Haven

La Belle · · Clewiston

HENDRY

LEE

Bonita Springs ·

Naples ·

Marco Island ·

COLLIER

Southwest

INTRODUCTION

Southwest Florida Backroads Travel is your mentor to Southwest Florida and some of the most diverse country in the state. You will find old Florida country towns with hardworking cowboys and fishermen, and also some unbelievably rich towns populated with famous people. It is a vast land of beaches, high rise condominiums and wealthy golf course communities.

It stretches from the white sandy beaches of Englewood in the north to the marshy fishing villages of Everglades City and Chokoloskee in the south. There are more golf courses in Southwest Florida than you can shake a putter at. The area also has great fishing and boating. The region has experienced tremendous population growth in the past twenty years, but Old Florida can still be found on the backroads.

There are only 5 counties in Southwest Florida: **Charlotte, Glades, Lee, Hendry** and **Collier.** The Southwest Florida road map above will help you plan your travels.

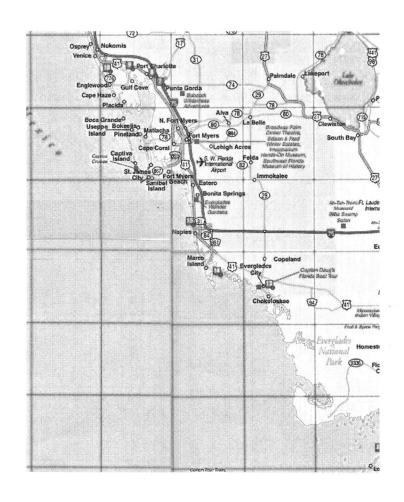

TOWNS AND CITIES

Southwest Florida Backroads Travel lists places to stay and eat on the individual town pages. The individual town pages include a brief history of the town along with my recommended motels, hotels and restaurants.

The towns and places in this guide include the following:

Alva

Ave Maria

Boca Grande

Captiva Island

Fort Myers

LaBelle

Marco Island

Moore Haven

Naples

Old Naples

Palmdale

Punta Gorda

Alva

Alva is not so much a town as it is a place. It is about 11 miles east of I-75 on State Road 80 between Fort Myers and LaBelle. People who live in Alva say it is more than a place: it is a state of mind. From I-75, take Exit 141 and head east on State Road 80 toward LaBelle. After about 11 miles you will come to a little crossroads called Alva. A convenience store on the north side of the highway is your landmark. Turn left at the flashing light and cross the old bridge over the Caloosahatchee River. Turn right on Pearl Street, and you are in the heart of Alva.

History of Alva Florida

A lot of people assume the town got its name for a famous nearby winter resident: **Thomas Alva Edison**. This is not the case, however. A sea captain from Denmark named **Peter Nelson** came up with the name. He bought a large tract of land and laid out the original village in the late 1800's.

Captain Nelson admired a small white flower that grew in the area. It turned out our sea captain was also a botanist, and he recognized the flower as **The Alva Flower**, also known as sabatia brevifolia Rafinesque. He naturally named his little Florida town for the Alva Flower.

The first bridge across the Caloosahatchee was built at Alva in 1903. It became quite a busy little town, with a couple of hotels and several houses. Like many Florida towns of that era, its life revolved around the river.

I first noticed Alva while crossing the state of Florida on the **Okeechobee Waterway**. A friend and I were moving my sailboat from Coconut Grove to Punta Gorda. The Okeechobee Waterway connects the east and west coasts of Florida. The Caloosahatchee River is the western part of this connection.

After a long day on the river, we passed under the Alva drawbridge toward the end of the afternoon. We spent the next couple of nights at **Rialto Harbor**, 2 miles west of the Alva Bridge. It was more than a marina; it was an Old Florida experience. The family who owned Rialto Harbor lived on the property. In addition to a few boat slips, they had an Old Florida style cottage for rent.

The grounds were plush with many plants and animals including a horse. They were friendly folks, and built a campfire each night for everybody to sit around and tell stories. The guest cottage was beautiful, but more expensive than I like to pay for a night's lodging. It would be perfect for a family who wants to spend a few days there. I'll never have a chance to stay in that cottage because Rialto Harbor closed its doors after our visit. It was a great place to visit and I wish it were still there.

There is no shopping district in Alva, but it does have a nice little church and a museum. The museum sign says it is open on Saturday from 2-4 P.M. You have to admire a Florida town whose museum is open only one day a week.

There is a nice boat launching area and parking lot just east of the church. This is a very busy place on winter weekends. This entire stretch of the Caloosahatchee River could use a few more boat launching locations.

The homes in Alva are simple and modest with the exception of one large new house on the river. The biggest building in town is a nearby elementary school. There is a nice clean adult mobile home community at the end of Pearl Street.

The entire area around Alva enjoys large oak trees with lots of hanging moss. Alva doesn't quite fit in as one of the Florida ghost towns that are fun to visit. After all, people still live here. But it certainly is quiet. I recommend Alva as a place to relax and watch the boats go by.

ALVA MOTELS

Your best bet is back at the interchange on I-75. No place to stay in Alva unless you want to camp at nearby **Caloosahatchee Regional Park**, 18500 North River Road Alva, FL 33920. Tel: 239-694-0398

Ave Maria

Ave Maria owes a lot of its existence to **Dominos Pizza**, the huge franchise operation that promises to deliver your hot pie within 30 minutes. The founder of Dominos, **Tom Monaghan**, was the leader of the effort that brought this beautiful new town into existence seemingly almost overnight.

Ave Maria is a planned town near **Immokalee**, about 25 miles east of Naples. The community was established in 2005 by a partnership of **Barron Collier Companies** and the **Ave Maria Foundation**. The foundation was led by Tom Monaghan, who reportedly invested $250 million in the new town and its university.

Ave Maria and its University

The principal institution of the new town is **Ave Maria University**. Mr. Monaghan served as its first president until he stepped down in 2011. This is a private Catholic university that was formerly in Ypsilanti, Michigan until it closed in 2007. Ave Maria School of Law is an accredited American Bar Association law school, and has a current enrollment of 375 students.

Ave Maria University today has more than 1,000 students and was recently ranked one of the **Top Ten Colleges in Florida** by **USA Today**. Monaghan's vision is for the school to have more than 5,000 students one day and have athletic teams in the NCAA Division 1.

The university, law school and surrounding residential communities are arranged around the carefully planned town center of Ave Maria. The focal point of the town center is the **Ave Maria Oratory**, a large steel framed structure that serves as both church and university chapel. The Oratory was inspired by a Tom Monaghan sketch that captured his long time interest in the work of Frank Lloyd Wright.

The initial development of the residential communities around Ave Maria was slowed down by the real estate crash of 2008 and beyond, but more homes are being built and the downtown can be an interesting and busy little place. There is a restaurant, a pizza place, a coffee shop and a small number of other establishments.

The downtown around the Oratory has been designed with apartments and condominiums above the shops so that residents can enjoy a walkable lifestyle. If I were a professor at Ave Maria University, I'd think one of these homes would be a great place to live.

AVE MARIA RESTAURANTS

The Pub & Grille At Ave Maria, 5068 Annunciation Circle, Ave Maria, FL 34142. Tel: 239-867-4235.

Milanos Pizza of Ave Maria, 5080 Annunciation Circle, Ave Maria, FL 34142. Tel: 239-867-4296.

AVE MARIA HOTELS

Your best bet is to book a hotel in Naples, about 23 miles west of Ave Maria. Here is one suggestion:

Hampton Inn I-75 Naples, 2630 Northbrooke Plaza Drive, Naples, FL 34119. Tel: 239-596-1299.

Boca Grande

Boca Grande is a place that most Floridians have never visited. It's at the end of the road, just like Key West, but far less known. It has some of the same quirkiness and bohemian nature that is typical of Key West and other Florida end of the road towns. Boca Grande is at the southern end of State Road 771.

You need to find your way to Placida, Florida by taking State Road 776 from Port Charlotte or State Road 775 from Englewood. The roads intersect at Placida.

A toll bridge takes you from Placida to Gasparilla Island and Boca Grande on SR-771. Pay the $6 toll and go into an interesting and charming part of Old Florida.

History of Boca Grande Florida

Boca Grande is on Gasparilla Island. **Gasparilla** was the nickname of Jose Gaspar, the "last of the buccaneers", a famous pirate. Jose may have been fictitious. Nobody knows for sure. Google him and have some fun. There are many versions of who he was and what he did. Real or not, he is the inspiration for **Tampa's annual Gasparilla Festival**.

The first residents in the area were Calusa Indians, who lived on nearby **Useppa Island** as long ago as 5,000 B.C. and on Gasparilla Island by 800 or 900 A.D. Charlotte Harbor was the center of the Calusa Empire, a hunting and fishing tribe which numbered thousands of people and hundreds of fishing villages. The first contact the Calusa had with the white man came during Spanish explorations at the beginning of the 16th century.

By the mid-1700s the Calusa had all but disappeared, the victims of European diseases, slavery and warfare.

Just like the Indians, the earliest settlers came to Gasparilla Island to fish. By the late 1870s several fish ranches were operating in the Charlotte Harbor area. One of them was at the north end of Gasparilla Island in the small village called Gasparilla.

The fishermen, many of them Spanish or Cuban, caught huge numbers of mullet and other fish and salted them down for shipment to Havana and other markets. In the 1940s the Gasparilla Fishery was moved to Placida across the bay, where it still stands today, and the fishing village died out.

Many of the early fishing families of Boca Grande are represented in third, fourth and even fifth generation descendants who still live in the area.

Quite a few old homes remain. The one above is the **Anchor Inn**, a bed and breakfast.

Phosphate and Tarpon made Boca Grande Florida famous. In 1885 phosphate rock was discovered on the banks of the Peace River just north of **Punta Gorda** on the east side of Charlotte Harbor. Phosphate was a valuable mineral for fertilizers and many other products, and was in great demand worldwide. This discovery transformed the south end of Gasparilla Island into a major deep water port because Boca Grande Pass is one of the deepest natural inlets in Florida. Barges loaded with phosphate came down the Peace River and Charlotte Harbor to Port Boca Grande. There the rock was loaded onto ocean going freighters.

Wealthy sportsmen also discovered the Charlotte Harbor area for its fantastic fishing and hunting. It became famous as a great place to catch tarpon, a fighting game fish.

In 1905 the phosphate producers decided to build a railroad to Port Boca Grande. Phosphate would come by rail rather than barge. The only buildings on south Gasparilla Island at this time were the lighthouse and house at the southern tip of the island.

By 1907 the railroad was completed along with a 1,000 foot long pier at the railroad terminus. For the next 50 years The Charlotte Harbor and Northern Railroad carried phosphate to Port Boca Grande. The trains were off-loaded directly onto ocean going freighters for delivery to ports all over the world.

By 1969 **Port Boca Grande** had become the fourth busiest port in Florida. Although it was a commercial town, its centerpiece was still the **Gasparilla Inn**, pictured below.

The railroad connected Boca Grande Florida to the world. The **Charlotte Harbor and Northern Railroad** not only brought phosphate and supplies to Gasparilla Island; it also brought wealthy people from the north.

By 1910 Boca Grande Pass was already famous for its unequaled tarpon fishing among fishermen, who stayed on nearby Useppa Island. The **Agrico Company**, having begun to see the potential of the idea of developing Gasparilla Island beyond the port, began to develop the village of Boca Grande.

The railroad station in what would become downtown Boca Grande was built. The company also built streets, sidewalks, streetlights, shops, a post office, and water and telephone service. The town was landscaped, including the famous section of Second Street called **Banyan Street**. The railroad company built several cottages downtown and a few wealthy families from "up north" purchased land and built winter residences.

The train stopped at Gasparilla, the fishing village at the north end of the island, at the railroad depot in downtown Boca Grande, and at the south end phosphate terminal.

In 1929 the **Boca Grande Hotel** was built just south of downtown Boca Grande. It was a three-story, brick resort hotel where most of the island weathered the hurricane of 1944. The Boca Grande Hotel changed hands and was demolished in 1975. It took six months to raze the building by means of fire and the wrecking ball, as it had been built to withstand fire and hurricanes.

The railroad continued to bring the grand visitors from all along the eastern seaboard until the **Boca Grande Causeway** opened in 1958.

In the 1970s phosphate companies increasingly switched their interest to ports in Tampa and Manatee County. As more money was spent developing these ports, traffic to **Port Boca Grande** began to dwindle. The railroad continued to run trains to the south end until the phosphate port closed in 1979. The depot was restored and a number of shops, offices and a restaurant now occupy the old building. The **Gasparilla Island Conservation and Improvement Association** transformed the old bed of the railroad into Boca Grande's popular Bike Path.

Boca Grande has become a unique community, with a large number of wealthy winter residents rubbing elbows with the fishermen and other locals. Tarpon tournaments are held in Boca Grande, and there are many charter fishing boats with knowledgeable captains.

Former **President George H. W. Bush** is one of many famous people who have spent many winters at the **Gasparilla Inn**.

Locals remember President Bush's wife Barbara and dog Millie, and their spirited grand-daughters Jenna and Barbara.

Britt Hume of FOX News vacations in Boca Grande and broadcasts some of his reports from there.

BOCA GRANDE HOTELS

Gasparilla Inn & Club, 451 Gilchrist Ave, Boca Grande, Florida 33921. 941-964-2201. This has been a premier destination on Florida's Gulf Coast since 1913. It is on the National Register of Historic Places. Stay in one of the beautiful rooms in the main hotel during season or in a guest cottage during the summer months.

The Anchor Inn, 450 4th St, Boca Grande, Florida 33921. 941-964-5600. Four nice units in a clean old Cracker style inn.

BOCA GRANDE RESTAURANTS

Eagle Grille & Miller's Dockside, 220 Harbor Drive, Boca Grande, Florida 33921. 941-964-8000. Tasty dining overlooking Boca Grande Marina. The Grille's main dining room and screened porches have great views of the marina, bayou and Charlotte Harbor.

Loose Caboose, 433 W. Fourth Street, Boca Grande, Florida 33921. 941-964-0440. The Loose Caboose is located in the historic train depot in downtown Boca Grande. They serve fresh local fish and produce in a comfortable, family atmosphere. A large patio area for outside dining lets you watch the world go by. Interior dining room is air conditioned.

Pink Elephant Restaurant, 5th & Bayou Avenue, Boca Grande, Florida 33921. Boca Grande, FL 33921. 941-964-0100. This is a fine restaurant associated with The Gasparilla Inn and Club. It is a short walk from the inn. This popular restaurant is open Tuesdays through Sundays. Collared shirts and slacks are required upstairs, but less formal island casual wear is acceptable downstairs.

Temptation, 350 Park Avenue, Boca Grande, Florida 33921. 941-964-2610. This fine restaurant reminds me of some of the places in the Florida Keys.

BOCA GRANDE ATTRACTIONS

Gasparilla Island State Park. This park is located at the southern end of Gasparilla Island, just south of Boca Grande. You can visit the historic Boca Grande Lighthouse Museum and enjoy the beach.

Gasparilla Inn is on the National Register of Historic Places. It has been beautifully restored and is worth a stay or just a trip to the lobby for a good look.

Captiva Island

Captiva Island is immediately north of Sanibel Island just west of Fort Myers. It fronts the Gulf of Mexico on the west and Pine Island Sound on the east Captiva and Sanibel used to be joined until a severe hurricane in 1926 separated them by creating a new channel to the Gulf known as Blind Pass.

The old legends say that Captiva is named because the pirate **José Gaspar**, also known as **Gasparilla**, held his female prisoners on the island. Historians can't confirm that Gaspar really existed, but it makes for a colorful story. Another interesting story is the history of the **Tween Waters Inn**, a resort that is on the **National Register of Historic Places** and is still a great place to stay.

Wilbert Herbert Binder first homesteaded Captiva in 1888. His grave is in a small cemetery next to **The Chapel By The Sea**. The chapel is a small white wooden sided little church on the beach.

It welcomes people of all spiritual beliefs, and is open from Thanksgiving to Easter every year. That's the time of year everybody on this island calls **"season"**.

Captiva is accessed from Sanibel by a small bridge over Blind Pass, and Sanibel is reached by a toll bridge connected to the mainland west of Fort Myers. Until this bridge was built in the 1960s, access was by car ferry from the mainland pictured below.

Captiva Road heads north from Sanibel to the very northern end of Captiva Island. It is a canopied trail with occasional views of the beautiful blue Gulf and white sand beaches. The luxury homes along Captiva Road are known as **"Millionaire's Row"**. These homes are both on the Gulf of Mexico and the bay to the east. The small area known as **Captiva Village** is at the north end of this road just before it enters the **South Seas Island Resort and Yacht Club**.

The Village is the heart of local life on the island. There are art galleries and boutiques, a small library and the chapel mentioned earlier. There are several restaurants, and quaint homes tucked away among bright tropic flowers and palm trees. Captiva Drive runs east-west in the Village and connects the boat docks of Pine Island Sound with the Gulf of Mexico white sand beach.

Captiva Island has taken its share of hurricane damage over the years. The most recent was **Hurricane Charley** in 2004 that damaged or destroyed more than 300 buildings on its way to smashing into **Punta Gorda** on the mainland.

The **South Seas Island Resort and Yacht Harbor** occupies the northern two miles of Captiva Island. It was built on the site of a large key lime plantation many years ago and suffered extreme damage from Hurricane Charley in 2004. It is now completely restored after a $140 million renovation, and is a mainstay of the island economy.

THINGS TO DO ON CAPTIVA ISLAND FLORIDA

There are several small businesses on Captiva that offer a wide range of adventures. Among these are kayak eco tours, day sails and boat trips to nearby **Useppa Island and Cabbage Key** where Jimmy Buffett got the inspiration for **"Cheeseburger in Paradise"**. Some of these businesses operate out of South Seas Resort, Tween Waters Inn and Captiva Village.

Shelling both on Captiva and nearby Sanibel is also a favorite thing for many visitors.

RESTAURANTS ON CAPTIVA ISLAND

Green Flash, 15183 Captiva Dr, Captiva Island, FL 33924. Tel: 239-472-3337. A great place for fresh seafood. They have swordfish, shrimp, grouper, sea bass and other specialties when available. Great view, and the sunsets are special. You might even see the famous "green flash" when the sun sets over the Gulf.

Old Captiva House, 15951 Captiva Drive, Captiva Island, FL 33924. Tel: 239-472-5161. This restaurant is located at the Tween Waters Inn. Upscale dining on a laid back island, but very good food. Waiters in tuxedo shirts, entrees pretty expensive. Seafood delicious and well prepared. Great place to catch a sunset.

Sunshine Seafood Cafe, 14900 Captiva Dr, Captiva Island, FL. Tel: 239-472-6200. Good local seafood nicely prepared. Excellent sea bass and paella. A good wine list and a place where the locals love to eat.

CAPTIVA ISLAND HOTELS

Vacation Rentals by Owner and other rental agencies have listings for privately owned houses and condos on Captiva Island. There are also a few fine lodging establishments on the island.

Captiva Island Inn Bed & Breakfast, 11509 Andy Rosse Lane, Captiva Island Florida 33924. Captiva Island Inn is unique with several small cottages scattered around the Captiva Village area. Each one is close to the restaurants, entertainment and shops in the heart of the Village, and is an easy walk to the beach. Average rates $135-$207.

Jensen's On The Gulf, 15300 Captiva Dr, Captiva Island Florida 33924. This is a small luxurious facility with several small cottages and condos on the beach in Captiva Village. It has no pool or other resort amenities, but it is next to a wonderful beach and is a short walk from all the restaurants and other attractions in the Village. They also have **Jensen's Twin Palms Cottages and Marina** on nearby Pine Island Sound with cottages, boat rentals and a charter fleet. Average rates at Gulfside $175-$700, at twin Palms $120-$200.

South Seas Island Resort and Yacht Harbor, 5400 Plantation Road, Captiva Island Florida 33924. South Seas is on the far north end of the island and is a self-sufficient vacation destination. It is a gated resort with rooms, villas, private homes and condos available for rent. The resort has several swimming pools, a marina, restaurants, tennis courts and a 9 holes golf course, the only golf course on the island. The resort has car rental facilities, a grocery market and deli and a fitness club. Average rates $161-$389.

Tween Waters Inn, 15951 Captiva Road, Captiva Island, FL 33924. This inn is located at the skinniest part of Captiva Island about a mile south of the village area of Captiva. It has several vintage rooms, cottages and efficiencies with views of the bay and the Gulf. It also has a swimming pool and tennis courts, a marina and a restaurant called the Captiva House. The Gulf beach across from the inn is one of the best on the island. The entire resort was placed on the **National Register of Historic Places** on December 15, 2011. Average rates $130-$222. .

Fort Myers

Fort Myers is in the southwest part of the state south of Tampa and Sarasota and north of Naples. It is located on US-41 and is near several I-75 exits. State Road 80 also comes in from West Palm Beach on the east coast.

History of Fort Myers

The area around Fort Myers is thought to have been visited twice by Juan Ponce de Leon's expeditions in 1513 and 1521. Southwest Florida saw sparse habitation in the 16th and 17th centuries, occasionally seeing Spanish fishermen and pioneers who set up temporary encampments on the barrier islands and coast. In the 1700s, San Carlos Bay and Charlotte Harbor became popular spots for Caribbean pirates looking to careen their ships for maintenance and tally their booty. The presence of the Spanish and its status as a hangout for buccaneers made the spot notable enough for British cartographers to put it on their 18th century maps.

When Florida became a US Territory in 1821, protection for Florida's influx of settlers and entrepreneurs soon became a priority for the federal government. Unfortunately for this effort, Florida already had inhabitants, the Seminole.

A conglomeration of Muskogee tribes, escaped slaves and other refugees, these resourceful natives had been pushed out of their traditional homes in the colonies down into Florida's mangroves and subtropical forests.

For years they had found peace and sanctuary in this dense and desolate wilderness. The Seminole would not give up their new home without a fight, and the US government had not forgotten the Seminole's vengeful raids across the border while Florida flew a British flag. Thus began the **Seminole Wars**.

By 1850, the newer settlers were starting to clash with Seminoles in the south. A spot along the Caloosahatchee River was chosen for the site of the first base of operations in what came to be as the **Third Seminole War**, known as **The Revenge of Billy Bowlegs**. The first fort of many to come in Southwest Florida, Fort Myers was named after **Colonel Abraham C. Myers**, whose father-in-law was the commander of Ft. Brooks in Tampa. With the surrender of Chief Bowlegs in 1858, the last major Seminole threat in Florida was removed.

Fort Myers Florida in the U.S. Civil War

From 1863 to 1865, the fort was occupied by the Union. It was the site of the Civil War's southernmost battle when a small contingent of rebels failed to capture the fort. Ironically, the fort's namesake Abraham C. Myers was serving in the Confederate Army at the time in the unenviable position of CSA Quartermaster General.

After the Civil War had ended, the fort lost all strategic value. It was soon dismantled for materials by the crackers and cattle ranchers living on the Caloosahatchee plains. As the Confederate battalion that attacked Fort Myers had been comprised of local ranchers, one has to wonder if perhaps the fort's dismantling wasn't just about easy money. Regardless, some of the first structures in Ft. Myers were built with timber taken from the dormant outpost. In 1885, the Town of Ft Myers FL was incorporated.

Thomas Alva Edison built his winter home, Seminole Lodge, in the new city. For a time the inventor was Ft. Myers' most notable resident. Edison was instrumental in the development of Fort Myers when he wasn't conducting experiments in his lab at the Lodge.

Near the turn of the century, the unfortunately named Tootie McGregor and the Edisons began a beautification project in the city. The team trucked in Royal Palms to be planted along picturesque Riverside Drive, now appropriately called McGregor Boulevard. It would have been fun if they had named it Tootie Trail instead.

Some of those original palm trees still line the street, many reaching heights of 75 feet. Fort Myers is home to so many varieties of palms and subtropical plants that it's nicknamed **"The City of Palms"**.

Thomas Edison's friend, Henry Ford, visited Edison at home and was so impressed he built his own winter home next door. Other prominent friends came too, like Harvey Firstone.f

With the construction of the lush **Royal Palm Hotel** in 1898, Fort Myers became a major destination for the rich and famous. Its excellent fishing and warm Gulf waters enhanced its reputation.

Major construction projects brought jobs and growth to the city. The construction of the Tamiami Trail Bridge across the Caloosahatchee River in 1924 brought the city's first real estate boom. Fort Myers was spreading like a wildfire. The happy days were not to last long for the city, though.

The real estate boom soon turned into a bust as the country entered the **Great Depression**. While the city struggled, federal works projects did manage to bring some aid.

The **Works Progress Administration** brought Ft. Myers the Edison Bridge, Yacht Basin and the Parthenon-like Federal Post Office building.

Fort Myers During World War Two

As with many cities in America, World War II revitalized the local economy. Ft. Myers came full circle, once again becoming a military outpost with the arrival of the Buckingham Field and Page Field air bases. While they were saving towns in Europe, our service men and women were also saving towns in America with their dollars. The thousands of military personnel brought Ft. Myers back from the dead with their business and the government contracts that came with them.

Fort Myers has grown from a small cowpoke town to a major tourist destination with **Boston Red Sox** and **Minnesota Twins** training camps.

FORT MYERS RESTAURANTS

Lighthouse Restaurant & Bar, 14301 Port Comfort Rd, Port Sanibel Marina, Fort Myers, FL 33908 - (239) 489-0770. Beautiful marina view and live entertainment.

Thai Star, 6611 Orion Drive, Unit 106, Fort Myers, FL 33912.- (239)-208-4057. Great Thai food. Owner Bill and his wife continue the fine dining tradition they started in Bonita Springs.

FORT MYERS HOTELS

Sanibel Harbor Resort & Spa, 17260 Harbour Point Drive, Fort Myers, FL 33908 - (888) 896-1959. Go here if you really want to treat yourself or your family. Located on its own private peninsula overlooking beautiful San Carlos Bay. Spa treatments and more amenities than you can shake a stick at.

Comfort Inn & Suites. 10081 Intercom Dr., Ft Myers FL 33901 - (866)-538-0187. Reasonable rates, clean, close to the airport.

The Hibiscus House Bed and Breakfast, 2135 McGregor Boulevard, Fort Myers, FL 33901. Tel: 239-332-2651. This B&B is snuggled between the historic Edison-Ford Winter Estate and the Old Fort Myers Downtown area. It is within walking distance to the Caloosahatchee River, Centennial Park and many fine restaurants.

FORT MYERS ATTRACTIONS

Edison and Ford Winter Estates, 2350 McGregor Blvd., Fort Myers Florida 33901. Tel: 239-334-7419. The beautifully maintained winter homes of Thomas Alva Edison and Henry Ford still fascinate modern visitors.

Magic Wind Adventure Sailing, 2500 Main Street, Fort Myers Florida - (800) 975-5824. Join Captain Paul for a high seas adventure on their 38' sailboat, the "Star of Orion". 1/2 day or multiple-day outings are available.

Manatee Park, 10901 State Road 80 Ft Myers FL 33905 - (239) 694-3537. You're almost guaranteed to see a manatee here during the winter as they come in to escape the chilly ocean.

Imaginarium Hands-On Museum, 2000 Cranford Ave. Ft Myers FL 33901 - (941) 337-3332. Science museum and aquarium. The "hurricane simulator" will blow your socks off!

Day Trips to Sanibel and Captiva. Some of the most beautiful canopied roads and beaches are just a short hop over the bridge from Fort Myers.

LaBelle

LaBelle is the seat of government of Hendry County. The population of Labelle is just under 5,000. The town is located on the Caloosahatchee River about 18 miles east of Fort Myers at the intersection of SR-80 and SR-29.

Captain Francis Hendry, a civil war veteran of the Confederate army and pioneer Florida cattle rancher, named his new town for his daughters, **Laura and Belle**. Hendry County is named for him. In his time he was known as **"The Cattle King of South Florida"**.

Hendry began to build his cattle business after the Civil War. He made arrangements with a lot of cattle buyers in Cuba, and was one of the first ranchers in Florida to ship cattle there. He eventually owned 25,000 acres of fenced in grazing land and 50,000 head of cattle. His old home is open to the public and is a good example of how prosperous pioneers of the era lived. The home is on the National Register of Historic Places.

The old drawbridge downtown carries State Road 29 over the Caloosahatchee River and is a focal point for traffic in the area. There is a small city owned boat dock at the southwest corner of the bridge where a few boats can be accommodated at no charge for overnight stays.

There is also another marina on the northeast corner of the bridge with plenty of sailboats in storage.

Labelle has several good restaurants, and is the county seat of Hendry County. The courthouse and city hall are major employers in the area along with the agricultural industry. The Old Hendry County Courthouse was built in 1926 and is still in daily use. It's on the main drag at the corner of Bridge Street

(SR29) and Hickpoochee Avenue (SR80). The courthouse is on the **National Register of Historic Places**.

LaBelle hosts the annual **Swamp Cabbage Festival**, which is held in honor of the official Florida state tree - the cabbage palm - during the last full weekend of February. Here is a recipe for modern swamp cabbage from **Cooks.com**:

> **6 slices bacon, diced**
> **1/2 cup onion, chopped**
> **1-14 oz can hearts of palm**
> **1-16 oz can stewed tomatoes**
> **Salt and pepper to taste**

Saute bacon and onion until transparent. Add swamp cabbage, tomatoes, salt and pepper. Cook for 10-15 minutes. Good with fish or poultry.

LABELLE RESTAURANTS

Forrey Grill, 280 N Bridge St., LaBelle, FL 33935. Tel: 863-612-0423. Downtown near the bridge. Great food and atmosphere.

LABELLE HOTELS

LaBelle Motel, 170 W Hickpochee Ave., LaBelle, FL 33935. Tel: 863-675-2971. Downtown, clean and quiet, very inexpensive.

Marco Island

Marco Island is the largest and northernmost of Florida's 10,000 islands. It is about 28 miles south of Naples. For many years it was inhabited by the fierce Calusa Indians.

The first white settlers were **W. T. Collier**, his wife and their 9 children. They came to the island in 1870. In 1896, W. T. Collier's son, **Captain Bill Collier**, opened a 20 room hotel which still stands today, the Olde Marco Inn. This is not the same Collier family as the one that developed Everglades City and much of southwest Florida. That was **Barron G. Collier**.

Marco's early history was very quiet, but from 1908 to 1947 **the Doxsee Clam Company** was the biggest industry on the island. The company harvested, steamed and canned clams from the waters around Marco Island until the clam beds were exhausted.

After the clam cannery closed, **Barron Collier** bought most of the island from the other Collier family. There was almost no development on Marco Island. **This changed in 1964** when the **Deltona Corporation**, headed by the **Mackle Brothers**, began to develop the entire island as a beachfront resort and canal laced residential community.

The mangroves were removed from much of the island, and canals were dredged and the material used to create lots. It was a very successful project, in spite of some major permitting problems, and waterfront lots and homes were sold to eager buyers all over the world on the installment basis.

The 50 room **Marco Island Hotel** was one of the nicest in southwest Florida when it was built in 1965 at the same time the Marco Island community was officially opened.

Marco Island is now a modern place with some of the nicest condos and hotels in the state. From a quiet fishing village of 550 people in 1960, it has grown to a major town with a population of 16,000.

MARCO ISLAND RESTAURANTS

Snook Inn, 1215 Bald Eagle Dr, Marco Island, FL 34145. 239-394-3313. My favorite with great fresh seafood and a view of the pass from the Gulf of Mexico.

Le Be Fish, 350 Royal Palm Drive, Marco Island, FL 34145. 239-389-0580. Just about the best fish tacos you will ever had plus plenty of other seafood delights.

MARCO ISLAND HOTELS

There are so many nice hotels and vacation rentals available on Marco Island I suggest going to TripAdvisor or other travel websites for complete listings and review ratings. I like the **Marco Island Marriott** because it is right on the beach and is constantly being upgraded, but there are dozens more equally attractive options.

Naples

I lived in Naples for several years, and could dedicate an entire book to nothing but the town and its delights. In the far southwestern corner of Florida, many Floridians have never visited the town. It has only been fairly easy to reach by car in the past couple of decades with the extension of I-75 from the north.

The centers of present day life in Naples are the two historic business districts: **Fifth Avenue South** and **Third Street**. Great restaurants and shops abound in both districts, which are in the heart of what is known as **Old Naples**.

Downtown Naples and **Old Naples** feature many art shows and classic car shows in the season. **Cambier Park** is a local treasure in the heart of the city that has free movies every Saturday evening in season, and free band concerts every Sunday afternoon.

Free concerts are also held in the summers at the **Naples Beach Hotel and Golf Club**.

Downtown Naples also features the **Sugden Theater**, a community showcase for live plays, and the **Norris Center**, a smaller venue at Cambier Park for plays and small musical events. Von Liebig Art Center is on the northwest corner of Cambier Park. It features wonderful art exhibits all year long.

The **Pelican Bay** development just north of town features the **Philharmonic Center for the Arts** completed in 1989 at a cost of almost $20 million. The **"Phil"**, as locals call it, has a full program of music, dance and theater. Many traveling art exhibits also stop at the adjacent art museum.

Nature lovers will enjoy visiting the Everglades, whose nearest entrance is at Everglades City. You can explore the Everglades on foot or by canoe or airboat. You can even ride in a swamp buggy. Guided tours in these uniquely Naples machines are offered by Everglades Island Airboat Tours.

The **Naples Zoo** at Caribbean Gardens is also a favorite Naples attraction. The Naples area also has dozens of parks and wildlife preserves, and a world class botanical garden. The town has done a great job of preserving its historic residences and commercial buildings. Check out **Palm Cottage**, maybe the oldest building in Naples.

It's easy to just spend a complete day browsing the shops and restaurants on Fifth Avenue and Third Street. The ambience of the town has been carefully created and controlled over the years and it is obvious in the architecture and landscaping.

Naples is a very artistic community and has encouraged the display of art in public places. You will see wonderful statuary all along the main thoroughfares of Old Naples. There are also events staged at regular intervals along these business streets and music and refreshments are always available.

NAPLES RESTAURANTS

There are hundreds of great restaurants in the Naples area. I have one favorite.

Campiello, 1177 3rd St S, Naples, FL 34102. Tel: 239-435-1166. Great food, inside and outside dining, an elegant bar where everybody knows your name.

NAPLES HOTELS

There are hundreds of great hotels in the Naples area. The one below is a favorite that I've recommended to friends for years.

Trianon Hotel, 955 7th Ave South, Naples, Florida 34102. Tel: 239-435-9600. The Trianon Old Naples is a fine hotel featuring 55 spacious guestrooms and 3 large one bedroom suites, a heated pool and off-street parking. Guests enjoy a continental breakfast served daily in the lobby. The hotel is located in the residential neighborhood of Old Naples. Guests can walk to the waterfront area known as **"Tin City"** and to Downtown Naples and the Fifth Avenue Shopping District. Nearby is 3rd Street South and Cambier Park. The pristine beaches of the Gulf of Mexico are only 5 minutes away.

Naples History

The modern era of Naples history began when the town was founded during the late 1880s by **General John Stuart Williams** and **Walter N. Haldeman**. Williams was a former **Confederate general** known as John **"Cerro Gordo" Williams** for his exploits in the Mexican War. He also served with distinction in the Civil War. He became a United States senator from Kentucky after the Civil War. Haldeman was publisher of the Louisville Courier-Journal. The name Naples caught on when early promoters described the bay as **"surpassing the bay in Naples, Italy"**.

In the late nineteenth century, magazine and newspaper stories around the country featured many stories about Naples Florida.

These stories told about Naples history of balmy climate and abundant fishing and hunting. People began to hear about the little town. As a result of these stories, Naples began to develop a decent tourist trade.

Williams and Haldeman formed The Naples Company, and built a pier in the Gulf of Mexico and the **Naples Hotel**. These were the first significant structures in Naples history. Some of these buildings, along with the pier, still exist and are the focal point of **Old Naples** Florida , a beautiful historic neighborhood loved by residents and tourists alike.

The Naples Company struggled financially and finally went broke. It continued on in modest style under Haldeman's management. Haldeman built several cottages, and many of the early guests were friends or employees of Haldeman. Naples was a remote location in those days, but the fantastic hunting and fishing put it on the map. Henry Watterson, editor of the Louisville Courier-Journal, wrote in 1906:

"Naples is not a resort, but to the fisher and the hunter, Naples is virgin; the forests and the jungles are scarce trodden, the waters, as it were, untouched. Fancy people condemned to live on venison and bronzed wild turkey, pompano and sure enough oysters - and such turkeys! And such oysters!"

Naples was accessible only by boat in those days, and the town remained a remote winter retreat for rich northerners until the train came to town in 1927. This was the year before Barron Collier helped finance and push through the remaining link of the Tamiami Trail that connected Tampa with Miami. The dredge that was used to help build the trail can still be seen at Collier-Seminole State Park 17 miles east of Naples on the Tamiami Trail.

After World War Two, Naples Florida began to boom. **Aqualane Shores** was dredged out of the mangrove swamps just south of downtown and many waterfront lots were created. This neighborhood led the way for other upscale residential developments like **Port Royal** and **The Moorings**.

In 1959 the voters of Collier County decided to move the county seat from Everglades City to East Naples. The following year, 1960, saw Hurricane Donna with winds of 150 mph. The eye passed over Naples, Florida. No lives were lost, but there was massive destruction including the loss of the Naples Pier.

Growth since Donna has been steady, and Collier County was the fastest growing county in the U.S. for many years. Naples and surrounding Collier County now have more than 80 golf courses, many of them in gated communities.

The area has done a good job preserving and honoring its history. Near the restored historic Naples Pier is Palm Cottage, Naples oldest house built in 1895. Guided tours are offered in the winter season. Other historic buildings include the Naples Commissary Building in Olde Naples, dating back to 1903, and the renovated Naples Depot that dates back to 1927. The depot displays a caboose and other railroad memorabilia. It is also the location of one of Naples many annual automobile shows.

Naples history buffs will also find much of interest at the **Collier County Museum**, which houses a permanent collection from Prehistoric times through to the present day.

Old Naples

The neighborhood known as Old Naples does not have a precise definition, but I'll give it a shot here. I always think of the northwestern corner of Old Naples to be the **Naples Beach Hotel and Golf Club**. This was one of the earliest hotels in modern Naples, and is still a great place to stay. The locals love it for drinks at sunset. It is at the Gulf end of South Golf Drive (also known as 8th Avenue North.

Naples zoning does not allow any condos on the ocean south of the hotel, so there are only single family homes on the beach all the way down to the southern limit of Old Naples and beyond to **Gordon Pass** and **Keewaydin Island**. Some of these homes are bigger than many condominium buildings.

Old Naples is a charming combination of old beach cottages and mansions resting peacefully among hundreds of tall coconut palms and banyan trees. Some of the grand new mansions stand beside old cottages dating back more than 100 years. Every avenue, from **Golf Drive** on the north to **14th Avenue** on the south ends at the Gulf. These avenues each have little city parks with benches and are favorite spots for locals to watch the sunset.

The Southern Limit of Old Naples is 14th Ave S. The neighborhoods south of that, **Aqualane Shores** and **Port Royal**, are beautiful upscale communities that were dredged up out of the mangroves in the 1950's and are therefore not "old" by Old Naples standards.

The Old Naples I am describing is all west of U.S.-41 until the highway bends east and heads over to Miami as the famous Tamiami Trail. Then for the short section of US-41 that heads west before the bridge over the Gordon River, everything south of 41 and west of the Gordon River is Old Naples.

Tin City, a restored fishing village, is a local shopping venue on Gordon River that is in Old Naples.

Some people also refer to **"Olde Naples Florida"** (notice the e added to old), and that is generally the area around the Naples Pier and Third Street South

I lived in Old Naples from 2004 to 2010, and it will always rank as one of the nicest places I've ever lived. My small condo was two blocks from the shops and restaurants of Fifth Avenue South, and six blocks from the Third Street South historic district.

Palmdale

Palmdale is an unincorporated community located on US-27 in Glades County. **It is in this guide for those people that want to be as far from Florida civilization as possible**.

This lonely place is on high ground that marks the approximate southern end of the great sand ridge that forms the backbone of the Florida peninsula. It is where you jump off that ridge and drive west for many miles across prairies, palmetto scrub and ranch lands to the low lying Gulf of Mexico coast at Punta Gorda, or take State Road-29 down to LaBelle.

There may be no town or place in Florida that is further from the interstate highways than Palmdale It is in the middle of the huge agricultural land holdings of **Lykes Brothers**, one of Florida's oldest family dynasties. It is also located near the point where Big Fisheating Creek flows under US-27 on its way to Lake Okeechobee.

In the 1940's through most of the 1960's, US-27 was a heavily traveled 4 lane superhighway that funneled northern tourists down the center of the state. There were no interstate highways back then, or Florida Turnpike.

If you travel the highway today, especially south of Lake Placid and all the way down to Alligator Alley, you will see scores of old abandoned businesses. You will also see some of the old places still hanging on even though traffic is only a small shadow of what it was in its heyday.

The photo below by Mary Belland from the State Archives of Florida shows Tom Gaskins, who owned **The Tom Gaskins Cypress Knee Museum.**

This old attraction used to entertain tourists on both sides of US 27. The museum was on one side of the highway and the swamp catwalk and gift shop on the other. The museum displayed the bizarrely twisted "knees" that grow out of the roots of cypress trees.

The twisted cypress knees were made into signs to attract tourists and were nailed to trees and fence posts along US-27 for a couple of miles on both sides of the museum. The signs and the museum are missed by all who loved them.

There are still a few people who live in Palmdale, and there are signs along US-27 of busier times. Like this old building that offered rest rooms and liquor for travelers in the old days.

Palmdale may be in the middle of nowhere, but in this stressful busy age we live in that may not be all bad. The sky at night in this part of Florida seems to have more stars than the skies over the big cities along the coast. The silence is so quiet you can almost hear it.

You can't get any liquor or use the restrooms these days, but the Baptist Church is still serving local people down the road. A couple of things to do in Palmdale include:

Sabal Palm RV Resort & Campground. This privately owned small resort offers very reasonable rates for both full hookup and dry sites. They also have frequent music jam sessions along with a swimming pool and other amenities. It's a very quiet spot for camping.

Fisheating Creek Campground and Outpost. Is in the Fisheating Creek Wildlife Management Area. The campground has 120 sites, including RV sites, tent sites and primitive campsites. It is a good place to kayak and nature watch.

Gatorama Alligator & Crocodile Adventure is a couple of miles south of Palmdale on US-27. It is one of the oldest tourist attractions in this part of the state. It is a glimpse of Old Florida, and is still an appealing attraction that gets a fair share of visitors for a place so far off the beaten path. You can even order Gator meat if you are so inclined. I personally do not think it tastes like chicken; it's fishier.

Punta Gorda

The first thing you need to know about Punta Gorda is how to pronounce it. Forget your Spanish - native Floridians call it **PUNTA** (like punting a football). Don't say **POONTA** (although as Florida's influx of new people continues, this could change).

Punta Gorda has a population of about 17,000, and is the seat of Charlotte County. It is the only incorporated town in the County. Sprawling Port Charlotte, a huge General Development community on the north side of the harbor is not incorporated. The town gets its name from the Spanish term for the "fat point" of land where the Peace River meets Charlotte Harbor.

In the years after the Civil War, the Howard brothers came to the area and were the first settlers. About ten years later the railroad came to town, and Punta Gorda began to grow. The town was the end of the railway system, so a lot of tourists came down and stayed awhile. The town was incorporated in 1887.

Like many towns at the end of the trail, some tough characters settled there. There were reportedly 40 murders in Punta Gorda in the years 1890-1904. The town settled down as years wore on, and the shady characters either murdered each other or got respectable jobs.

The first bridge over Charlotte Harbor was built in 1921 to incorporate the new **Tamiami Trail (US-41).**

There are many historic buildings in Punta Gorda Florida, including the old Charlotte County Courthouse and 9 other places on the National Register of Historic Places.

Hurricane Charley came to town in 2004 and did a lot of damage. My sailboat was at Burnt Store Marina, south of Punta Gorda. Charlie came right over Burnt Store Marina. My boat lost her mast, bow pulpit and lifelines when a nearby boat pulled its dock pilings out and crashed into her during the storm's ferocious winds. A marina live aboard, after drinking too much beer, rode out Charley on his motorsailer. He took some amazing photos and videos and lived to tell about it.

The famous **downtown Indian** also survived, but the building it was next to did not and the Indian has been moved to another location in town. The storm sandblasted the red skin a pale shade of grey.

Downtown Punta Gorda is a pleasant destination with several good restaurants, some with outside dining. Other nice shops and restaurants are in **Fishermen's Village**, a rustic time share and shopping complex built out over Charlotte Harbor just west of downtown. **Punta Gorda Isles**, a large waterfront community west of downtown, has hundreds of waterfront residences, most of them having boats.

PUNTA GORDA RESTAURANTS

Punta Gorda has a wealth of restaurants, and so does Port Charlotte north of the bridge. Here are a couple of my favorites:

River City Grill, 131 W Marion Ave, Punta Gorda, FL 33950. Tel: 941-639-9080. Fine dining in downtown Punta Gorda. Noted for seafood, but great steaks too.

The Perfect Caper, 121 E Marion Ave., Unit 121, Punta Gorda, FL 33950. Tel: 941-505-9009. Gourmet dining and very popular with the locals.

PUNTA GORDA HOTELS

The Wyvern Hotel, 101 E. Retta Esplanade, Punta Gorda, FL. 33950. Tel: 941-639-7700. A nice new place right on the waterfront in downtown Punta Gorda. Close to restaurants and shopping.

Bokeelia Tarpon Inn, 8241 Main Street, Bokeelia, FL 33922. Tel: 239-283-8961. This inn is located at the northern tip of **Pine Island** overlooking the waters of Charlotte Harbor. It is an isolated location, but is a short car or boat ride to Fort Myers, Cape Coral, Boca Grande, Sanibel, Captiva, Punta Gorda and the Gulf of Mexico. Built in 1914, the house has been lovingly restored to retain the grace and comfort of the original home while providing today's amenities for guests. Each room has a queen bed with private bath and comes with evening hors d'oeuvres and wine plus a full breakfast each morning.

Useppa/Cabbage Key

Pine Island Sound is a shallow body of water lying west of the metropolitan area of Fort Myers and Cape Coral. Several romantic islands front on the sound, including **Gasparilla, Sanibel, Captiva, Useppa** and **Cabbage Key.**

Useppa Island has been the location of luxury resorts for more than 100 years, and is currently the location of the private **Useppa Island Club. Cabbage Key** is just across the sound, and is famous for the Old Florida restaurant that inspired Jimmy Buffett's song, **"Cheeseburger in Paradise"**. Both islands are only accessible by boat (or seaplane).

The origin of Useppa's name is shrouded in the mystery of this part of Florida that attaches to the pirate captain, **Jose Gaspar,** whose nickname was **Gasparilla**. The legend is that Gaspar kidnapped a Spanish princess named **Josefa**. He fell in love with her, but she would have nothing to do with such a nasty old pirate. So he imprisoned her on the island for the rest of her life. Or he killed her. History is vague on the subject, including whether or not Gaspar even existed. In any event, **Useppa** is supposedly a variation of the princess's name.

Long before the legend of the pirates, Useppa was a stronghold of the powerful native American Calusa tribe. Visitors today can still see evidence of the early settlements in the form of shell mounds and collections of various archeological digs. It is this archeological significance that placed Useppa on the U.S. National Register of Historic Places.

Useppa was purchased in 1894 by a Chicago streetcar millionaire named **John Roach**, who built a large winter home on the island. One of his guests was a wealthy New York advertising tycoon named **Barron Collier**. Collier bought the entire island from Roach and proceeded to develop much of southwest Florida, including completion of the famous **Tamiami Trail** from Naples to Miami.

He not only made Useppa Island his home, he turned it into a first class resort for the use of his friends and clients. Among his famous guests were many **Vanderbilts, Herbert Hoover**, many **Rockefellers** and **Rothchilds, and** celebrities like **Gloria Swanson, Shirley Temple** and **Zane Grey.**

The inn had several names over the years, including Tarpon Inn, Useppa Inn and Collier Inn. Time and hurricanes took their toll on the old resort, but the current owner has been steadily improving the club since buying it in 1976. It is now one again truly one of the most exclusive and elegant getaways in the United States. All homes are owned by club members, but seven guest rooms are available in the renovated hotel. Call 239-283-1061 for more information.

Cabbage Key Inn and Restaurant

Just to the west of Useppa is a small island called **Cabbage Key**. This island and its inn and restaurant can only be reached by boat There are several day cruises you can take if you don't have your own boat.

My preferred way of reaching Cabbage Key is to take a scheduled boat from **Pine Island Marina** and go out to the inn and restaurant at lunch. Pine Island itself is a worthy day trip by car.

A trip to Cabbage Key is the fun part of the trip; the food is okay, but nothing you would ordinarily drive this far to enjoy. Just enjoy the laid back ambiance.

Cabbage Key was a private home for many years before the inn and restaurant were opened in 1944.

The restaurant's main claim to fame is that it is reportedly the inspiration for Jimmy Buffet's great song **"Cheeseburger in Paradise"**.

There is outside and inside dining at Cabbage Key. The walls and ceiling of the inside dining room are festooned with thousands of one dollar bills, each bearing the name in magic marker of earlier diners. You will not feel complete unless you leave one of your own.

In addition to the famous cheeseburger, other typical tiki bar kinds of food are on the menu here. Plenty of seafood offerings including shrimp, salmon, crab craws, clam chowder and basic salads. Good black beans and rice complement many of the dishes. Sandwich varieties include mahi-mahi, grilled cheese, Reubens, and a lot of other simple fare. They have good cold beer. There are also several rooms and cottages for rent; it's a great place to spend a quiet day or two. The rooms are very basic. There is no cable TV out here on Cabbage Key, but plenty of water views. No swimming beaches on the island itself, but you can arrange to have a boat take you to nearby Cayo Costa with its abundant white sand beaches.

A trip to Cabbage Key reminds me of trips I've made to the Out Islands of the Bahamas. Don't expect five star hotel and dining experiences; just kick back, relax and enjoy being in a laid back place where time slows down.

BEACHES

The beaches of Southwest Florida are magnificent. From Marco Island on the south to Englewood on the north, these beaches are the envy of the world. Some of the better known beaches include the entire City of Naples, Vanderbilt Beach, Fort Myers Beach and Boca Grande.

Here are a few of my favorites.

Boca Grande. The island is not over developed with condominiums like much of Florida. You can enjoy miles of uncrowded beautiful sand beaches.

Captiva Island. Along with Sanibel, there are miles of white sand beaches. Some of them are loaded with sea shells, others are pure white sugar sand.

Delnor Wiggins Pass State Park, Naples. The beaches here are usually crowded only on weekends. Great walking and good swimming.

Lovers Key State Park, Fort Myers Beach. Sometimes very uncrowded on weekdays, more so on weekends. Beautiful clean beaches far from the nearest condominium.

Naples Beaches. Every east-west avenue in the City of Naples ends at a beautiful white sand beach with a dune crossover. Every one of them is among the best beaches in Florida.

Delnor-Wiggins Pass State Park
11135 Gulfshore Drive
Naples, Florida 34108
239-597-6196

Delnor Wiggins State Park is one of the most popular tourist attractions in Naples. The park's signature feature is its beautiful mile-long expanse of beach. Its official lengthy name is Delnor-Wiggins Pass State Park.

The beach's white sugar sand is punctuated by stretches of shell. It is usually voted as one of the best beaches in Florida. I agree, but may be prejudiced. This park is only one mile from where I lived for many years, and I was a frequent visitor. The park also features a boat ramp, fishing, swimming and picnicking. No camping is permitted.

ABOUT DELNOR WIGGINS STATE PARK

Younger folks may not remember who **"Bet a Million Gates"** was. John W. Gates lived from 1855 to 1911, and was a famous businessman. He was one of the founders of Texaco, and he was a barbwire millionaire on top of that. His nickname came from his compulsive tendency to gamble. Needless to say, he was a good gambler and ended up with $ 100 million when he died.

His favorite niece, **Dellora Angell**, inherited "Bet a Million's" fortune. She was only 10 years old. When she grew up she married **Lester J. Norris**. They spent their lives doing good things with the money. They donated millions for parks, hospitals, community organizations and other charities. They donated a lot of money to improve the existing park that was previously named Wiggins Pass State Park. The park was renamed in their honor: **Delnor**, for **Dellora Norris**. The other half of the name honors Mr. Wiggins, an early pioneer who lived near what is now **Wiggins Pass**. Delnor Wiggins State Park is a great name for a park. And now you know the rest of the story.

The beach is popular for sunbathing, swimming, beachcombing, snorkeling, and picnicking. Fishing is allowed at the north end of the park on the beach along Wiggins Pass. Swimming is not allowed in the fishing area. It's a great place to watch the famous Southwest Florida sunsets.

Sometimes Delnor-Wiggins gets overcrowded during the busy winter season. If this happens, the park closes its gates when it reaches maximum capacity.

PARK FEES

Fees are reasonable. $6. per car (up to 8 people), $ per car single occupant (August 2015).

HOURS OF OPERATION

Delnor-Wiggins Pass State Park is open from **8 a.m. until sundown** 365 days a year**, except if it becomes overcrowded**. An electronic sign at the **northwest corner of 111th Avenue and Vanderbilt Road** tells you whether the park is open or closed.

DIRECTIONS

Get off I-75 at Exit 111 in North Naples. Head west on Immokalee Road for about 5 miles. When you reach US-41, **Immokalee Road** changes names to **111th Avenue**. Keep going for another mile or so and you will run into the park.

STATE PARKS

There are 12 State Parks in Southwest Florida, some with great beaches. Some also have quiet campgrounds. All of them give you an opportunity to enjoy nature and see Florida the way it used to be. Any Southwest Florida travel experience will be enhanced by visiting one of these parks.

Here are addresses and telephone numbers for Southwest Florida State Parks. The parks that I've listed in **BOLD PRINT CAPITAL LETTERS** have full service campgrounds. Some of the others may have no camping at all, or primitive, equestrian or group camping.

Cayo Costa State Park, P.O. Box 1150 Boca Grande, FL 33921. 941-964-0375

Charlotte Harbor State Park, 12301 Burnt Store Rd., Punta Gorda, FL 33955. 941-575-5861

COLLIER-SEMINOLE STATE PARK, 20200 E. Tamiami Trail, Naples, FL 34114 239-394-3397

Delnor-Wiggins Pass State Park, 11135 Gulfshore Dr., Naples, Florida 34108. 239-597-6196

Don Pedro Island State Park, P.O. Box 1150 Boca Grande, FL 33921. 941-964-0375

Estero Bay Preserve State Park, 3800 Corkscrew Road, Estero, FL 33928 239-992-0311

Fakahatchee Strand Preserve State Park, P.O. Box 548, Copeland, FL 34137 239-695-4593

Gasparilla Island State Park, P.O. Box 1150, Boca Grande, FL 33921. 941-964-0375

KORESHAN STATE HISTORIC SITE, 3800 Corkscrew Road, Estero, FL 33928. 239-992-0311

Lovers Key State Park, 8700 Estero Blvd., Ft. Myers Beach, FL 33931. 239-463-4588

Mound Key Archeological State Park, 3800 Corkscrew Road, Estero, FL 33928. 239-992-0311

Stump Pass Beach State Park, P.O. Box 1150, Boca Grande, FL 33921. 941-964-0375

TOURIST ATTRACTIONS

There are dozens of tourist attractions in Southwest Florida. We will explore the following:

Babcock Wilderness Adventures

Big Cypress Loop Road

Edison and Ford Winter Estates

Naples Zoo and Caribbean Gardens

Most people agree that the biggest attraction of all in Southwest Florida is the spectacular sunsets. The beautiful blue backdrop of the Gulf of Mexico gives these sunsets their unique flavor. Look for the famous **"Green Flash"**.

Babcock Wilderness Adventures

Babcock Wilderness Adventures is one of the most unusual Florida tourist attractions. It takes place on a **92,000 acre working ranch** in the heart of **Old Florida**. Babcock Ranch is a working Florida ranch primarily engaged in raising beef cattle. The ranch also has large farming and mining operations.

The Babcock family of Pittsburgh owned the Babcock Lumber Company. E. V. Babcock came to southwest Florida in 1912 to hunt and fish. He liked the place so well he bought 100,000 acres of worked out turpentine pine woods and added to that acreage over the years. When most of the timber was logged out, Babcock converted the acreage to a cattle ranch.

When his son, Fred, was 14 he started coming to Charlotte County in the summer months to learn the cattle business. In the winters he worked in the family sawmill near Pittsburgh. Fred liked this lifestyle so much, he continued it the rest of his life - except that he wisely reversed the seasonal visits. He became one of the earliest snowbirds.

The ranch sprawls across Lee County and Charlotte County, and is northwest of Fort Myers and Punta Gorda. It is one of the last places in Florida where you may see the elusive Florida panther in its natural habitat. It is one of many possible surprises that have made this one the most popular Florida attractions.

You will also see the tough cows and bulls unique to the state known as Florida Cracker cattle.

Babcock Wilderness Adventures offers adventure-seeking visitors 90-minute Swamp Buggy Tours and a lot more. It takes about 2 1/2 hours to see everything on your Babcock Wilderness Adventures tour. The specially built shaded buggies carry you safely through native piney flat woods, oak hammocks, a fresh water marsh and a cypress swamp.

All told, you will see four different Florida ecosystems on your Babcock Wilderness Adventures tour. An experienced tour guide tells you all about the wildlife and explains the ranch activities and ranch history as well.

You will probably run into wild alligators and see hundreds of native birds on this tour. The ranch is also home to white tailed deer, wild turkeys, American Eagles and Red Shouldered Hawks. It is as close to nature as you can possibly be in Florida.

There is also a museum featuring Florida history, ranch operations, and natural history artifacts. There is even a movie set used in the **Sean Connery** film **"Just Cause"**.

You can also have a picnic at Babcock Ranch. You can bring your own picnic basket or enjoy a lunch of BBQ pork sandwiches, hot dogs and finger foods in the Gator Shack Restaurant.

The Babcock Ranch was sold not long ago to Kitson & Partners, a development company. The sale will probably not affect the future of Babcock Wilderness Adventures. The Kitson group intends to create a brand new city appropriately named **Babcock Ranch**. They donated all but 17,000 acres of the ranch to the state.

The remaining acreage will be used to create a futuristic, sustainable, environmentally sensitive community. It will be the first city almost any place on earth to use the sun for almost all of its energy needs

Who knows, this modern city could also end up being one of the popular Florida tourist attractions of tomorrow. Babcock Ranch (the new City) will have a state-of-the-art $ 300 million Florida Solar Power plant. The city will consume less power than the plant will produce. Most of the land adjacent to the new city will be preserved in its natural condition.

All tours are by reservation only, so it's best to call them before going. Please call 1-800-500-5583 for tour times or visit their website at www.babcockwilderness.com.

Big Cypress Loop Road

Big Cypress Loop Road is not on most lists of Florida tourist attractions, but maybe it should be. It is a lonely road about 27 miles long that parallels US-41 on its south side.

On Tamiami Trail (US-41) about halfway between Naples and Miami there was a ramshackle old building at a place called Monroe Station. It was built in the 1920's as a waystation, restaurant and boarding house for early travelers on the lonely stretch to Miami. The building sat abandoned for years, and every time I drove by I was amazed that it was still standing. It was only one hurricane away from being strewn all over the Everglades. It was finally destroyed by fire in 2016. It's blackened ruins mark the eastern entrance to Big Cypress Loop Road

There are two ways to travel on Big Cypress Loop Road. The first way and the hardest way is to take the partially improved

section of the Loop Road leading south from Monroe Station. Its official designation is CR-94. It heads south for several miles, and then bends east and north where it hooks up with Tamiami Trail again. The first 19 miles of this road can be rough going during wet conditions or if the surface has not been recently graded, but the average car will have no trouble in dry weather, but going slow.

Tamiami Trail was opened in 1928, and the Big Cypress Loop Road opened about the same time. It is probably the loneliest 27 mile stretch of road in Florida. A few hardy pioneers used to live along this road. Most of them are gone, their homesteads purchased by the federal government when the Big Cypress was assembled as a national preserve.

If you drive this stretch in a conventional car, the going has to be slow because of the wet spots, rough spots and potholes. They say in the old days it would take 3 hours to drive those 27 miles. I drove it recently in a Toyota Corolla in 1 hour and 20 minutes. Part of going slow was that I wanted to see the natural scenery.

Another way to see Big Cypress Loop Road is to enter the road from the eastern end near the Miccosukee Indian headquarters and give your car or truck or bike a break on the nice paved road. The eastern entrance to the Loop Road is at **Forty Mile Bend** on Tamiami Trail just west of the Miccosukee Indian headquarters building. It's called Forty Mile Bend because it's 40 miles from downtown Miami.

The first thing you will see are some nice concrete block houses on your left where some Indian families live. Shortly after that, the road gets lonely but it's easy driving. You may see alligators, bears, panthers and a human now and then. The humans are generally fishing in the numerous shallow streams and swampy areas. You won't see many signs of civilization, but will get a good feeling for how primitive life must have been in this wilderness for the early pioneers.

I like to play the country favorite **Orange Blossom Special** as I go through this lonely country. This is in honor of the late **Ervin Rouse**, who lived on the Loop Road some years ago. He is famous for writing the country music classic that's been recorded by hundreds of musical artists. In his later years he got by playing fiddle at local juke joints in the Glades.

He sold the rights to the song for peanuts and never made any real money from perhaps the most famous of all country music songs.

After about 8 miles this paved section ends at a Big Cypress ranger station and a trail head that will give you a great walking experience through the Big Cypress Swamp. Near the ranger station and still on the paved road, you will come to an interesting collection of old motorcycles, trailers, a tall wooden fence, firewood for sale, and a Lucky Strike sign. Sometimes this place is open to the public and it's a visit you should make if you are out on the Big Cypress Loop Road anyway.

This is the home and studio of **"Lucky Cole, Everglades Photographer"**. Maybe they call him Lucky because he has figured out a way to get beautiful women to pay him to photograph them in the nude.

Search for him on the internet and you will get a glimpse of his work. Like his neighbor down Tamiami Trail, **Clyde Butcher**, Lucky is a nature photographer. While Clyde is the Ansel Adams of black and white photographs of the silent beauty of the swamps and hammocks of the Florida Everglades, Lucky takes photos of another kind of natural beauty at his place on Big Cypress Loop Road. He appreciates the female form and is passionate about photographing women in their nude glory.

Lucky's place is a collection of weathered trailers, connecting decks and porches and a lot of interesting bizarre statuary and props that he uses in his photography business. Some of his photographs are on display at various locations around the property.

Lucky was raised in Miami Springs, and he and his wife **Maureen** moved to Big Cypress Loop Road in 1991. Lucky is familiar with the history of Big Cypress Road since he has been coming out to the area even as a boy. Lucky doesn't sell anything to tourists, but will give you a beer and sit and gab for a while. He does accept donations to his retirement fund.

When I visit him next I plan to bring some 12 year old scotch as a gift because I heard a rumor that he enjoys that as his favorite beverage.

You will enjoy sitting around the fire pit with Lucky and Maureen while he tells you about all the characters and gangsters that used to hang out on Big Cypress Road before the government bought most of them out. One of the gangsters that might get mentioned is the old **Scarface, Al Capone**.

In earlier times the Loop Road was the location of the village of **Pinecrest.** It was a logging town that grew to have about 200 people in the 1930's.

Pinecrest was also supposedly where Al Capone had a moonshining operation and gambling den that was operated by his cousin. Al also reportedly visited now and then from his winter home in Miami.

The only other residents of this lonely road today seem to be the Miccosukee Indians mentioned earlier who live in neat modern concrete block houses toward the eastern end of the 8 mile paved stretch. It's a very quiet stretch of Florida wilderness.

BIG CYPRESS LOOP ROAD LOCATION MAP

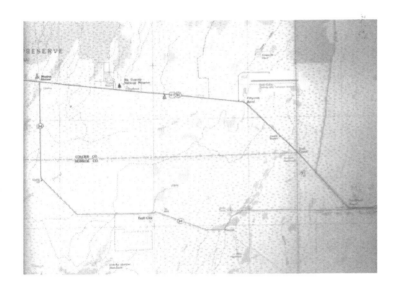

Edison and Ford Winter Estates

The Edison and Ford Winter Estates were tropical getaways for their famous owners, Thomas Edison and Henry Ford. Edison became one of our earliest Florida snowbirds. He bought property on the Caloosahatchee River in 1885, and a year later completed his vacation home. The Edison family named this place **"Seminole Lodge"**. Edison spent every winter here until he died in 1931.

Henry Ford was a good friend of Tom, and bought property next door in 1915. He built his winter home, called **"The Mangoes**, and spent many winters there.

Thomas Edison, Henry Ford and Harvey Firestone worked together for many years in Florida. Firestone became a frequent visitor to Fort Myers.

These two winter homes are large, rambling buildings that represent the best of old Florida. The homes are situated on 17 acres of landscaped lawn and gardens. Edison did much of his most important research and inventing while wintering in Fort

Myers. The large museum on site has hundreds of Edison and Ford inventions and other items.

The estates include botanical gardens with 500 unique plants, trees and flowers. They also have two "champion" trees and six former champions. The site also has a federal orchid program and a large greenhouse and nursery.

The Estates receive 225,000 visitors each year. It is one of the most popular Florida tourist attractions. It is also one of the 10 most visited national historic homes in the country.

Daily tours are conducted of the homes, museum, laboratory and gardens.

HOURS

Open Seven Days a Week 9:00 AM - 5:30 PM

ADMISSION FEES

Adults, $20. Children (6-12), $11. (May 2016)

Naples Zoo

Naples Zoo has been around in one form or another since 1919. This was the year when **Dr. Henry Nehrling**, a botanist and conservationist, bought the site to replace a plant collection he had in Central Florida that had been destroyed by a freeze. He figured Naples was far enough south he could start over and not be frozen out. He moved to the property and started a tropical garden that soon had 3,000 species of tropical plants. Many of them still remain on the zoo property.

The zoo continues its tradition of conservation by supporting projects all around the world ranging from endangered Florida panthers to Madagascar lemurs. The zoo is accredited by the Association of Zoos and Aquariums. It is a non-profit organization, having been purchased by the City of Naples after a record 73 percent of the voters supported the buy.

Naples Zoo has a wide variety of animals, many of them not native to this part of Florida. One native that has attracted a lot of attention, however, is a Florida panther named **"Uno"**. This animal was brought into the zoo for medical attention after it was discovered in bad condition in the wild after having been blinded by a shotgun blast. Uno has been patched up and is in good shape except for his bad eye.

Other animals live happily throughout the zoo in habitats to maximize their freedom and natural habitat. You will see alligators, anteaters, bears, cheetahs, snakes, foxes, frogs, gibbons, Gila monsters and a very popular honey badger that the kids love to interact with. The honey badger is behind glass and is one of the toughest little animals in the world, pound for pound.

Naples Zoo has many exhibits. There are monkeys to watch, hyenas, coyotes and many other animals in natural settings or in shows.

Children love to feed the giraffes - there is a small herd of them here. Most of the animals are in various featured exhibits around the park.

Some of these animals are:

> **Florida Panther**
> **Pythons**
> **South American Wonders**
> **Honey Badgers**
> **Alligator Bay**
> **Black Bear Hammock**
> **South African Lions**
> **Tiger Forest**
> **Cheetahs**
> **Giraffe Herd**
> **Leopard Rock**
> **Backyard Habitat**
> **Coyotes**

It is easy to spend an entire day at the Naples Zoo, especially if you attend one or more of the many scheduled shows.

GENERAL ADMISSION FEES
Adults: $19.95, children and seniors less (May 2016)

ZOO HOURS

900am to 500pm seven days a week

FESTIVALS

Southwest Florida art festivals are usually held each year in the winter season when most of the snowbirds are in the area. These shows are held in many towns on the Gulf coast, including Naples, Fort Myers and Bonita Springs. I have attended many of these festivals over my years in Florida, and have enjoyed every single one of them.

Here is a partial list of annual art festivals, art shows, folk festivals and other Southwest Florida outdoor events arranged by month.

JANUARY

Second Weekend
Cape Coral Festival of the Arts - Cape Coral

Third Weekend
Bonita Springs National Art Festival - Bonita Springs

Last Weekend
Naples Invitational Art Fest - Naples

FEBRUARY

First Weekend
Artfest Fort Myers - Downtown Fort Myers

Third Weekend
Naples National Art Festival - Naples

MARCH

First Weekend
Mercato Fine Arts Festival - Naples

Second Weekend
Bonita Springs National Art Festival - Bonita Springs

Sanibel Shell Festival - Sanibel Island

APRIL-SEPTEMBER No art shows reported.

OCTOBER

Second Weekend
Holidayfest and Craft Extravaganza - Port Charlotte

NOVEMBER

First Weekend
Bi-Annual Fine Art Show – Estero (Miromar Outlets).

Last Weekend
Naples Fall Fine Art and Craft Festival - Naples

Sanibel Fall Art Festival - Sanibel Island

DECEMBER

First Saturday
Annual Swamp Heritage Festival – Ochopee

HERITAGE AND HISTORY

Southwest Florida heritage and history begins with the early Native Americans, the Calusa, who lived in the area 12,000 years ago. Many of the early settlers in this area were cattlemen, ranchers, farmers and fishermen who came here from other parts of Florida.

Southwest Florida History

Thomas Edison put southwest Florida on the map. Southwest Florida history certainly began before Edison and his cronies took up residence in Fort Myers. And there was a little bit of action down in Naples and Everglades City before **Barron Collier** came along. But not much. The history of Southwest Florida is one of transformation because these men came to the area.

Thomas Edison loved Southwest Florida, and spent 40 winters at his home in Fort Myers. His buddies **Henry Ford** and **Harvey Firestone** also had places in Fort Myers, and the three of them collaborated on many business ventures. Edison worked on many of his major inventions in Fort Myers.

In the early days of Fort Myers, Edison offered the city free electricity for all of the streetlights if the city would pay for the lights. The city council turned down Edison's offers because they were afraid the streetlights would keep the cows awake at night.

Southwest Florida heritage and history has been impacted simply by the fact that these famous men chose to winter here. It gave the area tremendous national publicity.

Southwest Florida history covers some pretty diverse ground. You will find old Florida country towns with a cattle heritage, and some fantastically rich towns. Back in the 1920's Naples was reported to have 26 millionaires and 22 rum runners. Those were the days of Prohibition, and fast boats made the run from Cuban and the Bahamas to Naples.

Barron Collier came along and changed Southwest Florida history and his family is still part of Southwest Florida heritage. He was not as famous as Edison, Ford and Firestone, but he was a man of action and a self-made advertising millionaire. The State of Florida had long wanted to build a road connecting Naples to Miami, but didn't have the money to pull it off. Collier became the solution to the problem.

He purchased huge tracts of land in Southwest Florida. His first major purchase was in 1906, when he bought **Useppa Island** south of Boca Grande pass. The Collier Inn on Useppa is still an Old Florida masterpiece.

Collier saw the value of connecting Southwest Florida with the east coast of Florida. He worked a deal where he would finance the construction of a road from Naples to Miami. It wasn't until 1923 that he was able to start construction on the Naples to Miami section. In return for Collier's road building efforts, the State created Collier County out of the southern part of Lee County in 1923. It was the location of most of his vast land holdings. The descendants of Barron Collier are still the largest private land owners in Collier County.

Collier's road was named **Tamiami Trail**. It is that segment of US-41 that connects **Tampa** to **Miami**. It is the highway that finally opened southwest Florida travel to the rest of the state. It led to the discovery of southwest Florida by the people moving to Florida.

Of the eight rest areas with lodging and restaurants that Collier built along the Trail, only one survived into recent years. It was a dilapidated old wooden building at **Monroe Station**, a lonely outpost many miles east of Naples. It was finally destroyed by fire in April 2016 and all that remains is charred rubble.

According to **Wikipedia,** the Tamiami Trail took 13 years to build. It cost $8 million and used 2.6 million sticks of dynamite in its construction. The Tamiami Trail officially opened on April 25, 1928.

Unlike the east coast of Florida, and even Tampa, Southwest Florida did not participate in a big way in the 1920's real estate boom that finally collapsed in the aftermath of the two killer hurricanes. The 1926 Miami hurricane, and the one that followed in 1928, put a crashing stop to the frenzied land boom on the east coast.

In the years that followed, Southwest Florida remained one of the quietest and least known areas of the state. Southwest Florida heritage and history - at least in the twentieth century - reflect the **American Midwestern culture** more than any other area of the state. Although many mid-westerners stopped in Tampa and Sarasota, it seems more of them kept pressing southward to Fort Myers and Naples. In those days, US-41 funneled motorists directly down from Michigan, Wisconsin, Illinois and Indiana.

Today, Southwest Florida is a vast region of beaches, high rise condominiums and wealthy golf course communities. It stretches from the white sand beaches of Englewood in the north to the marshy fishing villages of **Everglades City** and **Chokoloskee Island** in the south. There are more golf courses in Southwest Florida than you can shake a putter at. The area also has great fishing and boating.

Southwest Florida Heritage Sites

Here is a list of 75 Southwest Florida heritage sites listed by county. The County Seat is also listed.

CHARLOTTE: Punta Gorda

A.C. Freeman House
Blanchard House
Charlotte High School
El Jobean Post Office and General Store
Florida Adventure Museum of Charlotte County
H.W. Smith Building
Old First National Bank of Punta Gorda
Praise Tabernacle Church
Punta Gorda Atlantic Coast Line Depot
Punta Gorda Residential District
Punta Gorda Woman's Club

COLLIER: Naples

5th Ave. South Association
Bank of the Everglades
Big Cypress National Preserve
Captain John Foley Horr House
Collier County Museum - Naples
Collier-Seminole State Park
Delnor-Wiggins Pass State Park
Fakahatchee Strand Preserve State Park
Historic Smallwood Store
Immokalee Pioneer Museum at Roberts Ranch
Keewaydin Club
Monroe Station
Museum of the Everglades

Naples Depot Civic and Cultural Center
Naples Historic District
Naples Nature Center
Palm Cottage
Plaza Site
Tamiami Trail Scenic Highway
Teddy Bear Museum of Naples

GLADES: Moore Haven

Moore Haven Downtown Historic District
Moore Haven Residential Historic District

HENDRY: LaBelle

Ah-Tah-Thi-Ki Museum
Captain Francis A. Hendry House
Clewiston Inn
Clewiston Museum
Clewiston Theatre
Downtown LaBelle Historic District
Forrey Building and Annex
Old Hendry County Courthouse

LEE: Fort Myers

Alva Elementary School
Boca Grande Community Center
Boca Grande Lighthouse Museum
Bonita Springs Elementary School
Buckingham School
Cape Coral Historical Museum
Cayo Costa State Park
Don Pedro Island State Park

Downtown Fort Myers

Dunbar Community School

Edison and Ford Winter Estates

Edison and Ford Winter Estates

Edison Park Elementary School

Fort Myers Beach Elementary School

Fort Myers Downtown Commercial District

Gasparilla Island State Park

Historic Railroad Depot

J. Colin English Elementary School

Koreshan State Historic Site

Koreshan Unity Settlement Historic District

Lovers Key State Park

Mound Key State Archaeological Site

Murphy Burroughs House

Museum of the Islands

Old Lee County Courthouse

Randell Research Center at Pineland

Sanibel Lighthouse and Keepers Quarters

Schoolhouse Gallery

Southwest Florida Museum of History

Terry Park Sports Complex

Tice Elementary School

Useppa Island Museum

Whidden's Marina

Williams Academy Black History Museum

DAY TRIPS AND SCENIC DRIVES

The Southwest Florida day trips recommended in this guide are designed to keep you off the busy roads. This area of Florida is quickly growing, and the north-south roads can get really jammed up, especially during tourist season of December - April.

I-75 is the north-south interstate in this region. It comes into Florida near Jasper and meanders down the center of the state until it starts veering west toward Tampa. It goes all the way to Miami and stays pretty close to the west coast in this region.

The interstate exits are crowded with gas stations, fast food restaurants and motels. You can travel the state quickly and easily on this highway (except during rush hours), but not see much scenery or real towns. The town signs you do see are usually a few miles from the downtown section. The fun begins when you get off the interstate and hook up with the less traveled roads.

There are many state and county highways off the interstate that offer better scenery and a look at real towns. In Florida, some backroads are even four-laned.

Here are a few Southwest Florida day trips that I recommend:

Port Charlotte to Boca Grande

SR-771 from Port Charlotte to Boca Grande. Not much to see until you get to the Gulf. The clearness and blue green water will impress you, and you will enjoy the quaint Old Florida charm of Boca Grande and the beautiful white sand beaches. About 27 miles.

Fort Myers to Iona

McGregor Boulevard from downtown Fort Myers south to Iona. Magnificent palms planted in the day of Thomas Edison. Fine old homes, including the Edison and Ford Estates. About 12 miles.

LaBelle to Immokalee

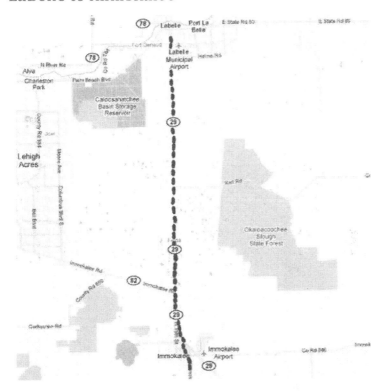

SR-29 from LaBelle to Immokalee. See how much of Florida is still grove and farmland. See how much is away from civilization, and enjoy the largely Mexican farm worker town of Immokalee. About 25 miles.

LaBelle to State Rd 31 on State Rd 78

SR-78 from LaBelle west to SR-31. Meanders along the north side of the Caloosahatchee River, huge trees, rural areas. Stop in Alva, not named after Thomas Alva Edison but a flower that grew nearby. About 21 miles.

Cape Coral to Matlacha and Pine Island

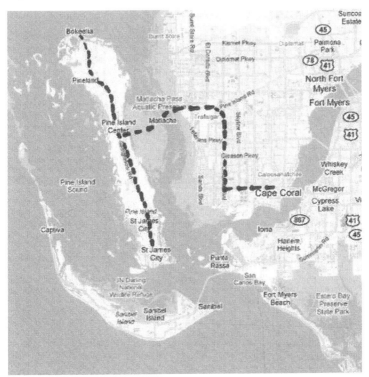

SR-78 (Pine Island Road) from Cape Coral to Pine Island through Matlacha. Up and down Pine Island on Stringfellow to Bokeelia and St. James City. A different kind of place. Home of author Randy Wayne White. About 50 miles.

Vanderbilt Beach to Gordon Pass

From Vanderbilt Beach Road in Naples south through Pelican Bay and Crayton Drive to the end of Gordon Drive in Port Royal. Then back to Third Street. The finest most expensive homes in Florida. About 12 miles.

Old Naples, Fifth Avenue, Third Street

Fifth Avenue in Naples. A redeveloped downtown area with fine dining and shopping. Extends from the Gulf across Third Street South to US-41. This is the heart of Old Naples.

Naples to Everglades City and Chokoloskee

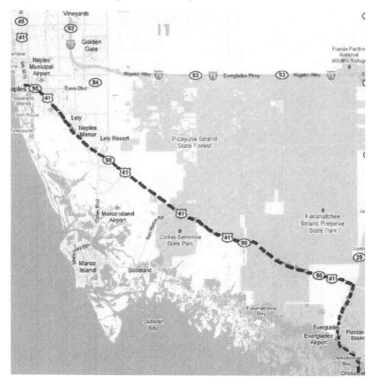

From Naples west on US-41 to State Road-29, then south to Everglades City and Chokoloskee. Lost in time, fishing village and low lands, airboats, mangroves and alligators. About 40 miles.

Tamiami Trail from Naples to Miami

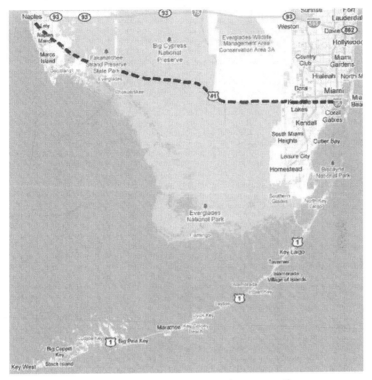

US-41 from Naples to Miami through the Everglades. Wilderness, Indian villages, scenic overviews. This stretch of road is called the Tamiami Trail, which actually extends from Tampa to Miami. In Miami it becomes Southwest 8th Avenue, the famous Calle Ocho. The lonely Big Cypress Loop Road can be a side trip on this stretch. Don't do this if it's been raining hard for hours. Both Tamiami Trail and Big Cypress road are likely to be flooded. The trip is about 108 miles.

EPILOGUE

Mike Miller has lived in Florida since 1960. He graduated from the University of Florida with a degree in civil engineering and has lived and worked in most areas of Florida. His projects include Walt Disney World, EPCOT, Universal Studios and hundreds of commercial, municipal and residential developments all over the state.

During that time, Mike developed an understanding and love of Old Florida that is reflected in the pages of his website, **Florida-Backroads-Travel.com**. The website contains several hundred pages about places in Florida and things to do. The information on the website is organized into the eight geographical regions of the state.

Southwest Florida Backroads Travel is based on the website. It is one of a series of eight regional guides that can be downloaded in PDF format or purchased as Amazon Kindle or soft cover books. If you find any inaccuracies in this guide, including restaurants or attractions that have closed, please contact Mike at Florida-Backroads-Travel.com and let him know. It is his intention to update the guide periodically and publish updated editions.

If you have enjoyed this book and purchased in from Amazon, Mike would appreciate it if you would take a couple of minutes to post a short review at Amazon. Thoughtful reviews help other customers make better buying choices. He reads all of his reviews personally, and each one helps him write better books in the future. Thanks for your support!

BOOKS BY MIKE MILLER

Florida Backroads Travel
Northwest Florida Backroads Travel
North Central Florida Backroads Travel
Northeast Florida Backroads Travel
Central East Florida Backroads Travel
Central Florida Backroads Travel
Central West Florida Backroads Travel
Southwest Florida Backroads Travel
Southeast Florida Backroads Travel
Florida Heritage Travel Volume I
Florida Heritage Travel Volume 2
Florida Heritage Travel Volume 3
Florida Wineries
Florida Carpenter Gothic Churches
Florida Festivals
Florida Everglades
Florida One Tank Trips Volume i
Florida Authors: Gone But Not Forgotten

80489776R00061

Made in the USA
Columbia, SC
07 November 2017